D0576882

NOW YOU CAN READ....
THE JOURNEYS OF ST. PAUL

STORY RETOLD BY LEONARD MATTHEWS

ILLUSTRATION BY MARK BERGIN

Library of Congress Cataloging in Publication Data

Matthews, Leonard.
  The journeys of St. Paul.

  (Now you can read—Bible stories)
  Summary: Retells the Bible story of Paul, who was
converted to Christianity by a miracle on the road
to Damascus.
  1. Paul, the Apostle, Saint—Juvenile literature.
2. Christian saints—Turkey—Tarsus—Biography—
Juvenile literature.   3. Tarsus (Turkey)—Biography—
Juvenile literature.   4. Bible stories, English—
N.T. Acts.   [1. Paul, the Apostle, Saint.   2. Bible
stories—N.T.]   I. Title.   II. Series.
BS2506.5.M38   1984   225.9'24   [B]   84-15129
ISBN 0-86625-315-7

Published by Rourke Publications, Inc., P.O. Box 3328, Vero
Beach, Florida 32964. Copyright © 1984 by Rourke Publica-
tions, Inc. All copyrights reserved. No part of this book may
be reproduced in any form without written permission from
the publisher. Printed in the United States of America.
  The Publishers acknowledge permission from Brimax
Books for the use of the name "Now You Can Read" and
"Large Type For First Readers" which identify Brimax Now
You Can Read series.

GROLIER ENTERPRISES CORP.

NOW YOU CAN READ. . . .

THE JOURNEYS OF ST. PAUL

When Jesus died, He left behind Him
many followers who truly believed in
Him. They were called Christians.
One man not only hated them, he was
always attacking them. Wherever he
went, Christians lived in fear. His
name was Saul. He lived in the city
of Tarsus.

In Jerusalem he hunted the Christians without mercy. He had many thrown into prison. Then one day he started on a journey to Damascus. With him he carried letters which gave him the power to round up any Christians he found there. Boldly he rode along followed by a few friends. Saul did not have many friends.

Little did Saul know that this was
to be the most important journey of
his life.

As he and his party neared Damascus,
Saul was suddenly surrounded by a
blazing light.

The light was so strong he had to
cover his eyes. He fell headlong to
the ground.

As he lay on the ground he heard a strange voice.

"Saul, Saul," said the voice sadly, "why do you always attack me?"

"Who are you?" cried Saul in a frightened voice.

"I am Jesus," came the voice again.

Saul began to shake with fear. He was too afraid even to open his eyes.

"What do you want with me?" he asked.

The voice of Jesus was stern.

"Get up and go to Damascus. There you will be told what you are to do."

Saul rose shakily to his feet. He opened his eyes. He reached out his hands.

"I cannot see," he cried. His friends had been watching him.

Saul's friends were afraid, too.
They had heard the voice of Jesus
but they had seen nobody.

Whispering among themselves, they
took Saul by the hand and led him
to Damascus. For three days he lay
there, unable to see. He did not eat.
He did not drink. He was waiting
and dreaming.

In his dreams, Saul thought he saw a strange man come to him. The man's name was Ananias. This man put his hand on Saul's eyes and Saul could see again. Now in Damascus there *was* a man named Ananias. He was a Christian.

One night Jesus came to him and said, "I want you to go to the street which is called Straight. There in the house of Judas is a man called Saul of Tarsus." Ananias was afraid. "Saul of Tarsus is our worst enemy," he said.

"I know," replied Jesus, "but I have chosen Saul for some special missions."

Ananias obeyed Jesus. Still, he could not help wondering. Why had Saul been chosen by Jesus? Ananias went to the house of Judas and asked to see Saul. He was shown in.

Saul welcomed Ananias excitedly.

"This must be the man I dreamed about," thought Saul. Ananias sat down beside Saul. Gently he put his hand on Saul's blind eyes.

"Brother Saul," said Ananias kindly. "Jesus has sent me to help you so that you may see again and believe in Him." At once something like scales fell from Saul's eyes. He could see again.

"Jesus has helped me," Saul cried. In this way he became a Christian. Never again did he attack anyone who believed in Jesus for Saul, too, now believed in Jesus.

Saul had not eaten or drunk anything
for three days. Now he got out of bed
and had a meal. Ananias went off to
tell other Christians about Saul.
They came to Saul and made friends
with him. He shook their hands.

Saul of Tarsus was no longer called Saul. After all, that was a hated name. With his new faith, Saul took a new name. Now he was known as Paul. He started to preach about Jesus in Damascus. The people of Damascus were amazed and angry.

What had happened to Saul? Why had he changed his name? Why was he, the enemy of Jesus, preaching about Him?

They listened to him in anger. Then, they started to hate him. They wanted to kill him. One night a big basket was lowered over the city walls.

The men who lowered the basket were
friends of Paul. In the basket was
Paul, escaping from Damascus.

When the basket touched the ground,
Paul climbed out and began to walk.
He walked a hundred miles to
Jerusalem.
There he found Peter, Barnabas and
other disciples of Jesus. When they
heard his story, they welcomed him.

Paul started to preach in Jerusalem. Before long he was in trouble again. Not everyone wanted to hear Paul's message. Some hated him.

Again, he had to escape. He went to Tarsus. Two years later he decided to take a trip to Cyprus with Barnabas.

Paul and Barnabas were teaching in Cyprus one day when a man tried to shout them down. He called Paul a liar. "Son of the devil," cried Paul. "How dare you try to turn these people against Jesus? Now God will punish you by making you blind."

The man was Elymas, a fake magician. He was thought to be a clever man.

Paul's listeners were shocked when they heard him suddenly cry out, "I cannot see! I am blind!" Elymas was blind for many days before he could see again.

When the ruler of Cyprus heard about this, he decided that he, too, must believe in Paul's faith. He was one of the first rulers to become a Christian.

This must have pleased Paul very much. He was soon off on his travels once more.

In the land we today call Turkey, Paul spoke to a man who truly believed in Jesus. The man had never walked in his life. "Stand up!" Paul ordered. The man did so and walked a few steps. The people who were there threw up their hands in wonder. Paul went on his way. All his life he travelled from one country to another, always spreading the words of Jesus.

Paul, the man who had once been the greatest enemy of the Christians was now their greatest friend.

All these appear in the pages of the story. Can you find them?

Ananias

Paul

basket

Barnabas

Elymas

Ruler of Cyprus

ship

Now tell the story in your own words.